1001

Really Ridiculously

SILLY JOKES

CLIVE GIFFORD

ILLUSTRATED BY
NIGEL BAINES

Hodder Children's Books

HODDER CHILDREN'S BOOKS

First published in Great Britain in 2018 by Hodder and Stoughton

3 5 7 9 10 8 6 4

Text and illustrations copyright © Hodder and Stoughton, 2018

The moral rights of the author and illustrator have been asserted.

A CIP catalogue record for this book is available from the British Library.

ISBN 978 1 44494 445 7

Typeset in ITC Franklin Gothic by Nigel Baines
Printed and bound in Great Britain by CPI Group (UK) Ltd, Croydon, CRO 4YY

The paper and board used in this book are
made from wood from responsible sources.

MIX
Paper from
responsible sources
FSC® C104740

Hodder Children's Books
An imprint of
Hachette Children's Group
Part of Hodder and Stoughton
Carmelite House
50 Victoria Embankment
London EC4Y 0DZ

An Hachette UK Company
www.hachette.co.uk

www.hachettechildrens.co.uk

CONTENTS

SILLY STARTERS

What was Batman put in prison for?
Robin.

Did you hear about the pizza party held in the world's smallest apartment?
Yes, the tomatoes left because there wasn't mushroom.

Why did the empty sandwich go to the dentist?
It needed a filling.

What do you call a 20,000 year old joke?
Pre-hysterical.

Dad: "Why are you typing that text message so slowly?"
Daughter: "Because my friend cannot read very fast!"

What is Prince William's favourite drink?
A cup of royal-tea.

What always sits in the corner but can travel round the world?
A stamp.

Doctor: "I'm afraid you have caught ancient Egyptian flu."
Sam: *"Who did I catch it from?"*
Doctor: "Probably your mummy."

What happened when the celebrity met fans at the river bank?
He gave out otter-graphs.

Why is Harry Styles terrible at singing songs backwards?
Because he likes to sing in One Direction.

Why was the policewoman hiding under a blanket?

She was working undercover.

Arjun: "I'm from India."
Freya: "Which part?"
Arjun: "All of me!"

What advice on table manners did Obi-Wan Kenobi give Luke Skywalker?

"Use the fork, Luke!"

Why did the well-behaved boy always sleep standing up?

Because he would never lie.

Patient: "I feel like I am both a yurt and a wig-wam."

Doctor: "Yes, that's because you've become two tents."

What's the difference between a nail and a rubbish boxer?
One gets knocked in, the other gets knocked out.

How did the fairy tale detective find his suspect?
He followed the foot prince.

What can you catch but not throw?
Your breath.

What title does the owner of the world's dullest company hold?
Chairman of the Bored.

"A time-traveller from 500CE Britain appeared on a singing contest last night."
"What instrument did he play?"
"An Anglo Saxon-phone!"

What is the longest night of the year?
A fortnight.

There once was a man from Roots Hall
Who went to a fancy dress ball
He thought for a gag
He'd go as a bag
But got carried away with it all!

Why could the pirates not play card games?
Because their captain was standing on the deck.

What did the policeman use when he arrested the naughty pig?
Ham-cuffs.

Harry: "Why is your luggage snoring?"
Carrie: "It's a knapsack!"
Harry: "Oh, I thought it was a sleeping bag!"

What did the policeman say to his own stomach?

"You are under a vest!"

How do you weigh a person who uses social media all the time?

In insta-grams.

Which British city do cooks visit to go camping?
Chef-field.

Wife: "Why is your back all covered in food?"
Husband: "Well, you told me to lay on dinner!"

What do you call a Transformer robot which lives at the bottom of the ocean?
Octopus Prime.

On which floor of the apartment block do Woody and Buzz Lightyear live?
The Toy Storey.

Why is the letter U like supper?
Because it comes after T.

What's the one thing you're guaranteed to get at your birthday?
A year older.

Knock, knock
Who's there?
Major
Major who?
Major answer a knock-knock joke!

What do policemen and women spread on their toast?
Traffic Jam.

What did the salad say when it went to church?
"Lettuce pray!"

What do you get if you cross a male goose and a martial arts expert?
Kung Fu Gander.

What newspaper do herbs read?
The Thymes.

Where did the cucumber hold its birthday party?
At the Salad Bar.

How many ears does a character in Star Trek have?
Three: a left ear, a right ear and a final frontier.

What gets wetter, the more it dries?
A tea towel.

Why did the Wild West outlaw turn and run when he faced the artist in a shootout?
He'd heard that the artist was good on the draw.

What was the name of the *Star Wars* character who slowly disappeared?
Darth Fader.

"Our local butchers is odd because it sells sweets."
"Really, what type?"
"Mints!"

On what day of the week does chocolate melt the most?
Sun-day.

What do you call a saleswoman who tries to charge you twice for the same thing?
Fifi.

Why did the DJ cover himself in itching powder?
So it would help him with his scratching.

"I hear that all TV detectives live in the same housing estate?"

"Really, what's it called?"

"Sherlock Homes."

How do you upset Lady Gaga?
Poke her face!

What do you get if you cross a famous children's book author with a seaside town?
Enid Brighton.

What is a pirate's favourite dinner?
Fish 'n' ships.

What rash did Harry Potter and Ron Weasley get after playing the school's flying broomstick sport?
Quidd-itch.

Knock, knock
Who's there?
Philippa
Philippa who?
Philippa bag with all your money – this is a stick up!

Why was the small rock braver than the big rock?
Because it was a little boulder!

How do you send a baby astronaut to sleep?
You rocket.

Patient: "Doc, I feel like a carrot and an onion..."
Doctor: "Well, don't get yourself in a stew!"

Why did the star go to school?
So that it could get brighter.

What did Gandalf say to Bilbo Baggins when he wanted him to leave?

"Hobbit!"

What do you call a girl who gets up at sunrise each day?

Dawn.

What do you call a man with seagulls on his head?

Cliff.

What do you get if you cross a painter with a judge?
A brush with the law.

Doctor: "How do you feel today?"
Patient: "With my hands, like any other day!"

What is Captain Underpants' favourite old movie?
Briefs Encounter.

Patient: "I've been acting like a goat, eating grass and climbing rocky slopes. Can you help me?"
Doctor: "When did you first feel like this?"
Patient: "Ever since I was a kid."

What happened to the King's chair?
It got throne away.

Why did the waiter put a skateboard under the chair of a dinner guest?
Because the customer had asked for a roll.

What do you get if you divide the circumference of an apple by its diameter?
Apple Pi.

What do you call a dentist who thinks deeply about things?
A flossipher.

What did Captain Picard say when a Vulcan threw a temper tantrum?
"Grow up and stop making a Spock-tacle of yourself!"

What sort of music are tortillas really good at?
Wrap.

Doctor, doctor, I feel like a ten pound note.
I prescribe a shopping trip. Go buy something, as the change will do you good.

What did the jar of mayo say when the boy opened the refrigerator?
"Close the door, I'm dressing!"

What's a showjumper's favourite country to compete in?
Horse-tralia.

What is a tornado's favourite party game?
Twister.

In the movie *Frozen*, why did Elsa's parents never teach her the whole alphabet?
Because they got lost at C.

What is a sergeant major's favourite month of the year?
March.

Did you hear about the fight at the chippie?
Yes, a fish and two sausages got battered.

What did Dec say when he entered his hotel room to find his TV partner wearing his boxer shorts?
"Ant's in me pants!"

Why was the undercover police detective spotted wearing a police uniform?
It was his day off.

I hear thieves stole all of your uncle's lamps. How is he?
Oh, he's de-lighted!

Knock, knock
Who's there?
Anita
Anita who?
Anita tow as my car's broken down.

What flies but never goes anywhere?
A flag.

Why was the policeman barbecuing meat in the garden?
Because he was ordered to prepare a stakeout.

What do policemen eat for breakfast when in a rush?
Cop-tarts.

How many ballroom dancers does it take to change a lightbulb?
"Five, Six, Seven, Eight!"

What is the best music to listen to when cooking a stir fry?
Wok and Roll.

Who did Sherlock Holmes call when he wanted to know which programmes were showing on the television?
Watson.

What were the snowmen doing in the garden on a winter's day?
Nothing much, just chilling.

TEACHER TITTERS

School Inspector: "How many teachers work in this school?"
Harry: "Oh, about a quarter of them, at most!"

Teacher: "Where was the Magna Carta signed?"
Chloe: "At the bottom!"

What's the difference between a really old teacher and a rhinoceros?
One's a grey, wrinkly, bad-tempered beast and the other has a horn and lives in Africa.

Teacher: "Why did the Emperor Nero have such a big empire?"
Mo: "Because he was always Roman around!"

Billy: "Sir, why does my maths book look so sad?"
Teacher: "Well, it's full of problems, Billy."

Why are chemistry teachers good at solving problems?
Because they have all the solutions.

Teacher: "Honestly, Jake, you should be thankful to the inventor of the zero."
Jake: "Yeah, thanks for nothing!"

Teacher: "Don't let me catch you mucking around again."
Emily: "I won't, Sir."
Teacher: "What?"
Emily: "I won't let you catch me!"

What's the difference between a teacher and a railway guard?
One minds the train and the other trains the mind.

What sort of lessons do witch teachers most enjoy?
Spelling.

Music teacher: "Which country produces most of the world's drumsticks?"
Olivia: "Is it Turkey, Sir?"

Maths teacher: "What is 2+2?"
Joshua: "If you don't know by now, Sir, I suggest you change jobs!"

Did you hear about the silly student teacher before his medical?
He spent hours revising for his blood test!

Teacher: "What sort of sandals do French men wear on their feet?"
Noah: "Phillipe-Flops."

Why did the teacher have a fish behind her ear?
It was her herring aid.

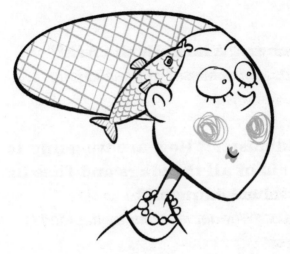

Teacher: "How many sides does a square shaped box have, Rosie?"
Rosie: "Two, Miss. The inside and the outside."

Teacher: "What are you doing in the scrapheap, Richard?"
Richard: "Sorry, Sir, I was hoping to find some junk food!"

How do Spanish language teachers get clean?
They take a bath-elona.

Teacher: "Who built the Ark?"
Dylan: "Sorry, Miss, I've Noah idea!"

Headmaster: "How are we going to get rid of all the slugs and flies in the school canteen?"
Sophie: "Why not let them try the food?"

Teacher: "You missed school yesterday, Emily."
Emily: "No, not really!"

Headmaster: "Mr Hanson, why are you running around your history classroom?"
Teacher: "I'm hoping to jog my students' memories."

Did you hear about the naughty witch girl who was always mucking around in class?
She got hex-spelled from school.

What did the Spurs-supporting teacher call his stick for smacking naughty children?
Harry Cane.

Did you hear about the boy with smelly armpits?
His teacher gave him a gold star for not putting his hand up in class.

Teacher: "Can you name a metal other than iron, silver or gold, Natalie?"
Natalie: "I don't zinc so, Sir."

Teacher: "Now, Tasha, why was the period of history called the Dark Ages?"
Tasha: "Was it because there were so many knights, Miss?"

Teacher: "Why have you bought a framed photograph of Queen Elizabeth II to your exam?"
Ethan: "Well, you told us to bring a ruler with us, Miss!"

What is the name given to a Spanish teacher who had his motor vehicle stolen?
Car-loss.

Amelia: "I wish I had been born 2,000 years ago."
Teacher: "Why?"
Amelia: "Because there would be a lot less history to learn."

Teacher: "Where's your report on time travel?"
Max: *"I'll work on it next month, Miss, and hand it in last term!"*

Career Teacher: "So would you like a job cleaning mirrors?"
Ajay: *"Yes, it's definitely a job I can see myself doing."*

Teacher: "What's an asteroid belt?"
Callum: *"Something the Solar System uses to keep its trousers up!"*

"I don't want to go to school. All the teachers hate me and the schoolboys all bully me."
"But you have to, Trevor, you're the headmaster."

What are a pirate's favourite school subjects?
Aaaaart and Geograaaaarphy.

Teacher: "Where were two of King Henry VIII's wives beheaded?"
Maryam: "Just above their shoulders!"

How do brainy schoolkids travel to their holidays?
On scholar-ships.

Jilly: "My cookery teacher doesn't like what I'm making."
Jenny: "Why? What are you making?"
Jilly: "Mistakes, mostly!"

Teacher: "Mrs Benson, I'm afraid your daughter is a constant troublemaker. How do you put up with her?"
Mrs Benson: "I can't. That's why I send her to school."

Maya: "You wouldn't punish me for something I didn't do, would you, Miss?"
Teacher: "Of course not, Maya."
Maya: "Phew! Because I haven't done my homework."

Teacher: "I told you to write a page long report about milk but this is only half a page."
Student: "Yes, Miss, it's condensed milk."

Teacher: "Your son really is a wonder child."
Parent: "Great!"
Teacher: "Yes, we wonder if he'll ever sit still and learn anything."

Schoolkid: "Miss, do you like my drawing of a flock of cows?"
Teacher: "Herd of cows."
Schoolkid: "Of course I have, Miss. I'm not stupid, you know!"

Did you hear about the silly science teacher?
He put airbags around all the computers in case they crashed.

Scarlett: "Sir, sir, my pen's run out."
Teacher: "Well don't just sit there, go and chase it!"

Teacher: "What mammal is the hottest and most deadly?"
Student: "A vole-cano!"

Teacher: "What's the most difficult part of a computer to fix?"
Student: "Is it the hard drive?"

What do you call a teacher who is always forgetting things and making errors?
Miss Take.

Mandy: "Your name is Annabel, so why does everyone call you Eileen?"
Annabel: "Because one of my legs is 20cm shorter than the other."

Teacher: "Poppy, I want you to name 10 Arctic animals."
Poppy: *"Easy, six walruses and four polar bears!"*

Maths teacher: "If nine people each give you £50, what do you get?"
Student: *"A new bike and a games console, Miss!"*

Why did the school teacher wear sunglasses?
Because her class was so bright.

Teacher: "What is the fastest-growing country in the world, Cerys?"
Cerys: *"It must be the Republic of Ireland, Sir."*
Teacher [puzzled]: "Why?"
Cerys: *"Because its capital city is always Dublin."*

Thomas: "I think my schoolteacher is in love with me."
Will: "Really?"
Thomas: "Yes, look at all these Xs she's put all over my exam paper!"

Penny: "Did you know there are salamanders that pretend to be dragons?"
Teacher: "Really?"
Penny: "Well, it said online that they terrorised a town in Asia and some were 10 metres tall."
Teacher: "That's nonsense. Salamanders never grow beyond 30cm. What you're reading is fake newts!"

Teacher: "Jimmy, why have you put wellies on top of the school computer?"
Jimmy: "Because it says it needs rebooting."

Teacher: "Do you know the 20th president of the United States?"
Niamh: "No, we were never introduced."

Teacher: "Now, class, why did Velociraptor and T-Rex eat raw meat?"
Isaac: "Is it because they didn't know how to cook, Miss?"

Molly: "I think I was electrocuted during school lunch."

Headmaster: *"How come?"*

Molly: "I dropped my fruit scone, stepped on it and a currant went up my leg."

Teacher: "What is found at the centre of gravity, Chloe?"

Chloe: "That's easy, Miss. It's the letter V."

Parent: "I'm worried that my son is addicted to his phone. I've tried hiding it, but he always finds it."

Teacher: "Why don't you put it in his schoolbooks? I know for a fact he doesn't touch them."

Teacher: "What are the Great Plains?"

Aarav: "That's easy...The Airbus A380 and the Boeing 747, Sir."

Teacher: "Shall I tell you a chemistry joke, class?"
Class: "Don't bother, Miss. It won't get a reaction."

Teacher: "Olivia, why do we rarely see antelope?"
Olivia: "Because ants aren't very romantic, Miss, and rarely get married."

English teacher: "In *The Lord of the Rings*, why is it so hard to enter the lair of Sauron?"
Henry: "Because there always seems to be one Mordor."

Teacher: "What's a fjord?"
Layla: "Is it a car made in Scandinavia?"

SCHOOL FUN
AND PUNS

Auntie: "How do you like school, Isabel?"
Isabel: "Preferably closed for the holidays, Auntie!"

Knock, knock
Who's there?
Teacher
Teacher who?
Teacher-self, I've had enough of you mucking around in class!

Student: "Nurse, my memory has suddenly become terrible."
School nurse: "Don't worry. Try to forget all about it."

Dinner Lady: "What three things can you not have for lunch?"
Student: "Breakfast, dinner and tea."

What school subject is the fruitiest?
History. Because it's full of dates.

School was closed for half term and the janitor was cleaning up hours after the lessons ended. He walked in to a classroom and found a 10 year old boy, sitting on his own.
"Why are you still here, it's the holidays now," **said the janitor.**
The boy replied, *"My mum says I've got to stay at school until I'm 16!"*

Which part of a school is full of untrue facts?
The Lie-brary.

At what school do you learn to make ice cream desserts?
Sundae school, of course!

Why are Alpha Centauri and the brightest boy at school similar?

They are both A Star.

Which country's schoolkids are the nicest?

Germany, because children there are known as kinder.

What's your fashion design teacher like?

She can be a sew-and-sew, but sometimes she has the class in stiches.

Mum: "How did you find school today?"

Sarah: "Easy, I just hopped off the bus and there it was!"

Knock, knock
Who's there?
Pecan
Pecan who?
Pecan someone your own size, you nutty school bully!

MATHS

Who is the knight that patrols the edge of a circle?
Sir Cumference.

Why did the maths teacher insist all her class wear glasses?
Because she said it improves di-vision.

How do you get really hot in a room shaped like an equilateral triangle?
You go into one of the corners where it's always 60 degrees.

How do pirates work out the area of a circle?
They use the formula, Pi Arrrrh squared.

Why did the maths teacher ban glue from her classroom?
So that her students didn't get stuck on a sum.

Teacher: "I am giving you a statistics grade of average, Eva."
Eva: "Oh, Miss, that's mean of you."

Why did the four 2s skip lunch?
Because they already 8.

Maths teacher: "Assuming the average weight, what does a 1.8m tall male butcher weigh, Kyle?"
Kyle: "Er, meat, Sir?"

What do female maths teachers wear under their blouses?
Alge-bras.

ENGLISH

Teacher: "Thomas, can you use the word 'underwater' in a sentence?"
Thomas: "Easy. My grades at school are underwater because they're below C level!"

Did you know, reading books whilst sunbathing can make you well-red?

Student: "Miss, which hand is best to write my essay with?"
Teacher: "Neither. It's best to write with a pen."

Teacher: "What does 'illegal' mean, Jimmy?"
Jimmy: "Is it a sick bird, Sir?"

Student: "Miss, I can't write my essay on an empty stomach."
Teacher: "Well, try writing on a piece of paper instead."

Teacher: "What is the dictionary definition of maritime?"
Michael: "It's the point in the day when a wedding occurs."

Knock, knock
Who's there?
Canoe
Canoe who?
Canoe help me with my English homework?

Teacher: "Helen, what is a myth?"
Helen: "Oh that's easy, Sir. It's a female moth."

HISTORY

What do Sir Lancelot and Sir Galahad wear in bed?
Knighties.

How do you make a Victoria Cross?
Steal her lunch.

Why did Queen Elizabeth I struggle to breathe?

She had no heir.

A young history student called Gail
Stole a sword, shield and suit of chain mail
She so wanted to fight
Everyone as a knight
But is now spending knight time in jail!

Who was the best police detective in the times of the Vikings?

Inspector Norse.

Why did Plato and Pythagoras dislike French fries?

Because they were cooked in ancient grease.

Why was Tutankhamun pleased with the hole in his pyramid?

He had always wanted a tomb with a view.

Knock, knock
Who's there?
Toot
Toot who?
Toot and come in, the Egyptian pharaoh!

Teacher: "Well, your history homework has improved, William. There are only eight mistakes here."
William: "Great!"
Teacher: "Let's now look at the second sentence."

SCIENCE CLUB

You cannot trust atoms. After all, they make up everything!

What chemical element is most attracted to policemen?
Copper.

And what chemical element is most in use at a dry cleaners?
Iron.

What award was given to the scientist who lost 30kg in weight?
The No-belly Prize.

"I tried to find my red blood cells."
"What happened?"
"My efforts were all in vein!"

What do scientists at the Large Hadron Collider have for lunch?
Fission Chips.

How much does it cost to buy a neutron?
There's no charge.

What is the blood type of a gloomy person?
b negative.

What do two electrical scientists say to each other when they meet?
"Watts Up?"

Teacher: "Please explain. What is H_2O_4?"
Emma: "That's easy, Miss. It's for drinking and washing with."

Headmistress: "I'm afraid Mr Jenkins, your science teacher, is off sick."
James: "Can't we helium, Miss?"

Teacher: "Can you think of a good joke about the noble gases, class?"
Class: "No, Sir, all the good ones Argon."

Knock, knock
Who's there?
Ammonia
Ammonia who?
Ammonia beginner, but could you teach me about chemistry?

GEOGRAPHY

What did the English Channel say to the North Sea?
Nothing, it just waved.

What do you get if you cross a Paris landmark with a dessert?
The Trifle Tower.

What country do most pirates come from?
Arrrrh-gentina.

What's the fastest country in the world?
Russia.

Knock, knock
Who's there?
Venice
Venice who?
Venice your dad home this afternoon?

Knock, knock
Who's there?
Norway
Norway who?
Norway am I telling you any more knock, knock jokes!

To which city do Iraqis go to boast about their deeds?
Bragdad.

Which country is most surrounded by sharks?
Fin-land.

MUSIC

Why did the police arrest the musician?
He got into deep treble.

What do music teachers use to remind themselves what they need to buy at the supermarket?
A Chopin Liszt.

Did you hear about the dog who was friendly but terrible at playing classical music?
Yes, his Bach was worse than his bite.

Why did the music teacher lift the lid of the school piano?
She was searching for her keys.

What sort of music do balloons most dislike?
Pop!

Teacher: "Why have you brought a ladder to choir practice?"
Schoolgirl: "So, I can reach the high notes, Miss!"

What does a brass band use to keep their teeth clean and white?
Tuba toothpaste.

What type of singing are *Star Wars* characters excellent at?
Yoda-lling.

Teacher: "Why are you eating the sheets of music, Johnny?"
Johnny: "I was trying to stave off hunger before lunchtime!"

COOKERY CLASS

How many eggs do you need to make a Paris omelette?
One is un oeuf.

Teacher: "Why is there water all over the floor, Vicky?"
Vicky: "Because my saucepan is full of leeks, Sir!"

Why do you have to be cruel in cooking class?
Because you have to beat the eggs and whip the cream.

Teacher: "What cheese is made backwards, Ruby?"
Ruby: "Edam."

What's a pastry chef's favourite TV show?
Game of Scones.

Teacher: "Now, we're going to cook the German sausages."
Paul: "But Sir, they're the wurst!"

What's white, round, smells of vinegar and giggles?
A tickled onion.

Words and Definitions
by Dick Shunerry

Watering The Planet
by Wayne Fall

Stringed Instruments
by Amanda Linn

Enjoy Maths Vol 1
by Al Geebra

The Books of Writer,
Leo Tolstoy
by Warren Peace

Teacher

What did the bogey say to the finger?

"Don't pick on me!"

What do you give an elephant with diarrhoea?

As much room as possible.

How do lice and fleas travel around your body?

Mainly by itch-hiking.

What did the tongue say to the diseased gums in court?

"You just can't handle the tooth!"

Diner: "Hey! Why has my burger got a footprint on it?"

Waiter: "Well, you did say, 'Give me a quarter-pounder and step on it!'"

What do you call a Roman leader with hayfever?
Julius Sneezer.

What do you get if you cross a wookiee with a toad?
Star Warts.

A man by the name of Bart
Created the world's biggest fart
He ate a bean stew
Left the gases to brew
Then blew off his pants with a start!

How did the gross boy take a bubble bath?
He ate three tins of beans.

What runs and smells at the same time?
Your nose and your feet.

What sausage gives you the most stomach gas?
A frankfarter.

Why do French people say, "Yes" when they go to the toilet?
Because they need a "Oui".

Why did the bank robber take a bath before his robbery?
So he wouldn't be a dirty criminal and could make a clean getaway.

Teacher: "Please use the word gruesome in a sentence, Karl."
Karl: "I didn't wash my feet for a week and gruesome mould on them!"

Why were the baker's hands stinky?
Because he kneaded a poo.

Did you hear about the schoolboy who didn't change his underpants or socks for six months?
Yes, I heard he's in a class of his own.

Why did the toilet roll get into the lift heading down to the ground floor?
It wanted to get to the bottom.

What's brown, smelly and travels through space carrying aliens?
A Pooh-F-O.

How does a girl with a cut on her leg get to hospital?
She takes a taxi scab.

Knock, knock
Who's there?
Courtney
Courtney who?
Courtney spiders or maggots, recently?

What kind of pants do clouds put on when the weather is stormy?
Thunderwear.

Where in Britain are human body parts stored for transplants?
Liver-pool.

What sort of Indian food comes with its own toilet?
A vinda-loo.

Why do you call your nose Netflix when you have a cold?
Because it is always streaming.

What kind of button can you not do up?
Your belly button.

Knock, knock
Who's there?
Carl
Carl who?
Carl a doctor, I've just swallowed a slug!

What happened to the giant monster gorilla who couldn't go to the toilet?
He became King Kong-stipated.

What do you call a louse that got inside Sir Galahad's clothing?
A mite in shining armour.

What's black, white and red all over?
A giant panda that's blushing because it farted in public.

Teacher: "What is a guillotine?"
Pupil: "It's a French chopping centre!"

What sound does a bell made of poo make when it's struck?
Dung!

How many stinky trainers does it take to make a room smell bad?
A phew.

"I found a small dog in my toilet bowl, the other day."
"Really?"
"Yes, I think it was a poo-dle!"

What sort of vehicle carries chopped off feet from the factory to the hospital?
A toe truck.

Tom: "My underpants are so big that I can pull them up to my neck."
Alex: "Wow! What do you call them?"
Tom: "A chest of drawers!"

Knock, knock
Who's there?
Watson
Watson who?
Watson your chin? It's really gross!

Teacher: "Hand your test tube containing oxygen to your classmate, Jimmy."
Jimmy: "Ohh, Sir, I've just passed gas!"

What did one lavatory say to the other at the end of the day?
"My, you look a little flushed!"

What happened when the naturist sat down on a plate of hamburgers?
He got sesame seed buns.

What country is full of viruses and bacteria?
Germ-any.

What's bright red and very stupid?
A blood clot.

Patient: "I think I have a bladder infection."
Doctor: "Hmmm. Urine grave danger."

Why can't you ever hear a psychologist going to the toilet?
Because the "p" is silent.

Teenager Tim walks into A&E with a mouldy sandwich in one ear, half a pork pie in the other and a chocolate bar stuck up his nose.
The receptionist says, *"What do you think the problem is?"*
Tim replies, *"I think I haven't been eating properly."*

What happened when the dirty burglar trod mud all over the carpet?
The police rushed to the scene of the grime.

What do you call a lady whose house has two toilets?
Lulu.

Why did the smelly bacteria wear miner's hats?
They were off to work in the arm pit.

What *Star Wars* character is green, slimy and snotty?
Bogey-Wan Kenobi.

What did the handkerchief say to the bogies when the boy blew his nose?
"Snot fair!"

Knock, knock
Who's there?
Hatch
Hatch who?
Urgh! You've just sneezed all over me!

What do you call a Roman gladiator who's had his arms and legs chopped off?
Unarmed and de-feeted.

"Do you know who's been on the computer?"
"My little brother did once, but now he uses the toilet like everyone else."

My feet really smell of cheese
I'm not sure if it's Cheddar or Brie
But when left to fester
They stink of red Leicester
"You're Em-mental, I'm calling the police!"

How do zombies greet a victim?
"Pleased to eat you!"

"Did you hear the joke about the cold virus?"
"No."
"I'd better not tell you. We don't want you to spread it."

Diner: "Waiter, waiter, there's a live fish swimming in my soup!"
Waiter: "I expect it's trying to catch the maggots, Sir."

A fitness instructor called Tim
Suffered from terrible wind
He belched and passed gas
Upset a young lass
And found himself sacked from the gym!

What happened to the skunk who forgot how to smell bad?
It faced ex-stink-tion.

What rank is the soldier that guards the smelly toilets at army camps?
Loo-tenant.

How do acne spots grow bigger and stronger?
They do 50 zit-ups a day.

What's worse than finding a maggot in your uneaten apple?
Finding half a maggot in your half-eaten apple.

Did you hear about the man who ate three chicken omelettes a day for a week?
When he finally went to the toilet, there was a fowl eggs-plosion.

What dessert is furry, has a crispy white topping but throws itself off of tables?
Lemming Meringue.

Why don't monsters like eating people who compete in the London Marathon?
They give them the runs.

Monster 1: "I made my specialty for dinner: a stand-up comedian's head on toast."
Monster 2: "Mmmm . . . It tastes a bit funny!"

Diner: "Waiter, I'd like a soup with maggots in it and a salad with two squashed flies."
Waiter: "Sorry, Madam, we can't serve you that."
Diner: "Why not? You did yesterday!"

What pantomime do scabs and sores like most?
Pus in Boots.

What happened when the football midfielder belched loudly?
The referee awarded a freak hic.

There was a young lady from Hyde
Who ate some green apples and cried
She felt really funny
As the fruit in her tummy
Made cider inside her insides!

What are vampires' favourite fruits?
Neck-tarines and blood oranges.

What martial art did the boy with the terrible body odour take up?
Kung Poo.

Patient: "Will this cream really clear up my spots, Doctor?"
Doctor: "I can't say, as I never like to make rash promises."

Doctor: "Open wide and say 'Ah'."
Patient: "Aaaaaaah, Ooooo, Eeeeeee, that hurts!"
Doctor: "Mmmm. It appears you have irritable vowel syndrome."

"I picked up a rotten old chocolate bar the other day. It was full of weevils and covered in flies."
"Aha, you've discovered life on Mars!"

Why was the warrior at the Roman Colosseum just like a lion who's had a female antelope for dinner?
He was glad-he-ate-her.

Why did the athlete take a whole packet of laxatives?
Because he thought the runs would improve his fitness.

Knock, knock
Who's there?
Dishes
Dishes who?
Dishes how I talk shince I loshed my teeth!

Why do Tigger and Piglet smell rotten?
Because they sometimes play with Pooh.

A man is at a posh dinner when he breaks wind.
Another man exclaims, *"How dare you break wind in front of my wife!"*
The first man replies, *"I'm very sorry. I didn't realise it was her turn!"*

FUNNY FAMILIES

Mum: "What do you think my son is going to be when he passes all his GCSEs?"
Teacher: "Oh, I reckon around 50 years old."

"Your sister has lovely long hair all down her back."
"Shame she doesn't have it on her head!"

Dad: "Why are you going to bed with a ruler under your pillow?"
Son: "Because I want to see how long I sleep!"

Father: "Why are you crying, son?"
Son: "My new trainers don't fit."
Father: "That's because you've put them on the wrong feet, you silly boy!"
Son: "But Dad, these are the only feet I have!

Little brother: "Have you ever seen an alien before?"
Big sister: "No, you're my first one."

Grace: "Grandma, have you finished your jigsaw of Italian food?"
Grandma: "No, I'm missing one Pizza the puzzle."

Why did your mum stop making doughnuts?
She became bored by the hole business.

Emma: "How do you make my stupid brother laugh on New Year's Day?"
Lisa: "I don't know."
Emma: "Tell him a joke on Christmas Eve."

Why has your dad got his head bandaged?
He was ironing when the phone rang.

"My brother is so bad at cooking that he put the cake in the freezer."
"Why did he do that?"
"Because the recipe said that the cake needed icing!"

Mum: "Hello, is this the greengrocers? I'd like a kilo of carrots for my son."
Greengrocer: "Sorry, madam, we don't do swaps."

There was a young Welsh son called Ioan
Whose money for odd jobs was owing
He cried, "Dad, of course,
If you don't pay, I'm forced
To tarmac the lawn and stop mowing!"

Mother: "Doctor, my son has swallowed all of his pocket money."
Doctor: "Put him to bed and see if there is any change in the morning."

Dad: "What would you do with a rotting cherry, Jessica?"
Jessica: "Give it cherry-aid!"

Grandpa: "Why are you staring at the can of frozen orange juice?"
Ella: "Because it says 'Concentrate' on the side."

Son: "Mum, this turkey dinner is horrible!"
Mum: "Well, you did ask for a fowl meal!"

What do you call an older brother with half a brain?
Gifted.

What are twins' favourite fruit?
Pears.

"I hear your big sister's taking you all the way to Iceland during half-term, so why the glum face?"
"Because after that, we're going to Tesco, Sainsbury's and then Aldi!"

Dad: "Why are you doing your multiplication sums on the floor, Elin?"
Elin: "You told me not to use tables."

Mum: "Why did you put a slimy toad in your little sister's bed?"
Son: "I couldn't find any slugs or dead flies."

Sophia: "My brother reminds me of the sea."
Gina: "Because he's wild and powerful?"
Sophia: "No, because he makes me sick!"

Daughter: "When did you start putting a pair of glasses over your phone?"

Mum: "Ever since it lost its contacts."

Kyle: "Can I have a budgie for Christmas?"

Mum: "No, Son, you'll have turkey like everyone else."

MY SISTER'S SELF HELP
BOOKSHELF

Don't Give Up On Your Dreams
by Percy Veer

Whoops, My Pants Keep Falling Down
by Lucy Lastic

Calm Down Your Life
by Fran Tikk

Want To Look Fabulous?
by Anita May Coover

The Problem Of Noisy Sleepers
by Constance Nawring

Plan For Future Problems
by Justin Kase

Pretend To Like People
by Faye Kinnett

88

Dad: "Son, let me explain how banking works."
Leo: "Don't bother, Dad, I've already lost interest."

What social media does your mum's mum use to stay in touch?
InstaGran.

"Did you hear about my silly auntie who set fire to her laptop computer?"
"No. Why did she do that?"
"She was trying to burn a CD."

Why did your sister cut a hole in her umbrella?
So that she could see when it stopped raining.

Why's your brother singing a lullaby to the medicine cabinet?
Because it contains sleeping pills.

Nathan: "Grandma, why have you stopped using your smartphone?"
Grandma: "It's far too expensive. Every time I plug it in, it says it's charging."

"My sister wants to be an archaeologist when she grows up but I think it's a terrible idea."
"Why?"
"Isn't it obvious? Her career would be in ruins!"

Brother: "I'm thinking of taking a summer job at the local zoo."
Mum: "What about the terrible smell?"
Sister: "I'm sure the animals won't mind."

Knock, knock
Who's there?
Doris
Doris who?
Doris locked, Mum, which is why I had to knock!

Son: "Why did my sister sprinkle sugar on her pillow before she went to sleep?"
Mum: "So she could have sweet dreams, dear!"

Mum: "What did you learn at school today, Amelia?"
Amelia: "Not enough, it turns out, as I have to go back tomorrow!"

Freddie: "I made a real bargain today. I got four suits for just a pound."
Uncle: "How did you manage that?"
Freddie: "I bought a pack of playing cards."

Mum: "Have you finished the washing-up?"
Son: *"Yup, er . . . you know that souvenir plate you were always worried would get broken?"*
Mum: "Yes?"
Son: *"Well, your worries are over!"*

"I hear your sister was only vegetarian for a day."
"Yes, it was a missed steak."

What do grannies order in Indian restaurants?
Nan bread.

Mum: "I've just had a letter from school. The headmaster is not happy with your appearance."
Daughter: *"How rude! I cannot help the way I look."*
Mum: "No, he means you haven't appeared in class all week!"

Brother: "You should work in the perfume industry when you grow up."
Sister: *"Why? Because I'm fashionable and smell nice?"*
Brother: "No, because you get up everyone's nose!"

Amy: "Doctor, my mother's sister has a very sore throat. Can you help?"
Doctor: "Of course, I'll prescribe a course of auntie-biotics."

Mum: "You need to visit the dentist about your broken tooth."
Son: "Oh, don't worry. I'll just stick it back together."
Mum: "How?"
Son: "With tooth paste, of course!"

Grandpa was told his face looks as red as tomato ketchup.
He took it as a condiment!

Brother: "Did you hear about the monster who ate a wookiee?"
Sister: "Yes, he said it was Chewie!"

Mum: "I hope you're sharing that pair of skis with your little brother, Rachel."
Rachel: "I am. He gets to use them going up the hill, and I get to use them coming down!"

Why did the dim dad connect the Christmas tree lights to the Christmas pudding?
Because he wanted a currant to flow through the wires.

Dad: "Julia, please come into the kitchen and help me fix dinner."
Julia: "Why, Dad, have you broken it again?"

A DIY dad from Peru,
Dreamt he was totally covered in glue
He woke with the feeling
He was fixed to the ceiling
He was stuck up as the dream turned out
true!

Abigail: "Granny, Tommy is so greedy! He's eating all of your raisins."

Granny: *"That's okay, I already sucked all the chocolate off of them."*

"My brother used to work in a car parts factory but quit."

"Why?"

"He said it was exhaust-ing and that he needed a brake."

Hannah: "Mum, this coffee tastes like mud."

Mum: *"Well noticed, Hannah, it was ground this morning."*

Sister: "Did you know many countries in Europe don't sell frozen food?"

Brother: *"Norway! I'll Czech that out at Iceland."*

Did you hear about the new TV show hosted by Tess Daly for Britain's most stupid brothers?
Yes, I believe it's called Strictly Come Duncing*!*

What do you call a sister with a pot of low fat spread on her head?
Marge.

Why is the silly dad wearing an anorak and a parka while painting the fence on a hot summer's day?
Because the instructions on the paint tin say you need two coats.

Liam: "Grandpa, why do you always wear loud socks?"
Grandpa: "So that my feet won't fall asleep."

Did you hear about Auntie Maria's latest holiday? She went on a river cruise in Egypt carrying dozens of ketchup bottles!

Yes, she wanted to explore the sauce of the Nile.

How do prisoners talk to their families?

Using cell phones, of course!

Why did Granddad paint his dentures navy blue?

He wanted to be a Bluetooth speaker.

Brother: "What two letters of the alphabet are bad for your teeth?"

Sister: "D, K."

What did the zombie mother say when her daughter played hide and seek with the boy next door?

"Stop playing with your food!"

Fixing Home Leaks
by Dwayne Pipe

Improving Home Security
by Al Arm and Belle Ring

Home Improvements by
Jack Uzzie and Paddy O'Doors

Why Is My House Damp?
by Rufus Lee King

Build Your Own Home Slowly
by Juan Brickatatime

DIY Toilets and Sanitation
by Sue Ridgepipe

Installing Home Heating
by Boyle Err and Ray D'Ater

DAD'S DIY BOOKSHELF

Why do bananas use sunscreen on holiday?
Because otherwise, they'd peel.

Which route should you never use to go trick-or-treating?
The psycho-path.

Where do Santa's helpers go for help when they're unwell?
The National Elf Service.

Why was the Easter Bunny grumpy about having to go out to entertain children?

It was having a bad hare day.

What is a foot doctor's favourite part of Christmas dinner?

The sage and bunion stuffing.

Where's the best place to shop for Halloween fancy dress?

A boo-tique, of course!

Did you hear about the silly police detective who was found at the beach?

He had been told to investigate a crime wave.

Where do eco warriors go on their holidays?

Greenland.

Two cruise ships, one carrying red paint and the other blue ink, crashed into each other. What happened to the passengers?
They were marooned.

Doctor, doctor, I cannot help cover my house in Christmas decorations all year round. What's wrong with me?
It seems you are suffering from a bad case of Tinsel-itus.

Annie: "How long were you on holiday?"
Rosie: "Oh, the same as usual, about 1.65 metres."

What do you get if you cross carol singers and a skunk?
Jingle Smells.

What game do ghosts most like to play at Halloween?
Hide and shriek.

Why did the Easter Bunny enjoy surfing, skydiving and climbing?
Because it was a fan of egg-streme sports.

What do they sing at a snowman's birthday party?
Freeze a jolly good fellow!

"My big brother is going on a gambling holiday in France!"
"Toulouse?"
"No, silly, to win!"

Why do skeletons like working on Halloween?
Because they often get a bone-us.

How do you hire a donkey on holiday?
You put a brick under each of its hooves.

"Hey kid, would you like to buy Rudolph and his brother?"
"No thanks, they're two deer."

What do you get if you cross Father Christmas with a killer shark?
Santa Jaws.

What board game fanatics often gather together at Christmas?
Chess nuts.

What do sheep like to do on their summer holidays?
Have a baa-baa-cue.

Why was the history teacher such a grouch at Christmas?
He didn't like the presents, only the past.

Ed: "Oh no, my Halloween pumpkin has a hole in it."
Dad: "Don't worry, we can fix it with a pumpkin patch."

Alec: "Why is the front of your car all covered in pictures of rabbits, chicks and chocolate eggs?"
George: "I wanted an Easter bonnet."

Idris: "I built a really cool igloo yesterday and as I finished, the sun came out and melted it."
David: *"That's really funny!"*
Idris: "Nah! Snow joke!"

Knock, knock
Who's there?
Wendy
Wendy who?
Wendy Easter Bunny coming?

What did the Easter bunny say to the carrot?
"It's been nice gnawing you!"

If Santa had a voucher for three tools from a garden centre, what would he pick?
Hoe, hoe, hoe!

What happened when parking wardens clamped Santa's sleigh?
He cried, "Yule be sorry!"

Amelie: "How did you find the weather in Majorca?"
Mary: "Easy, I just opened my hotel room door and walked outside!"

What did the bread rolls do on their summer holiday?
Not much, they just loafed around.

What do you call one of Santa's helpers if he wins the national lottery?
Welfy.

What do you call a girl who likes to sing Christmas songs?
Carol.

How do you keep the Christmas dinner locked up and safe?

You use a tur-key.

Two nervous friends went on a camping holiday to have a quiet, relaxing time, but they came home early.

The trouble was the holiday was too in-tents.

Did you hear about the couple who got trapped on a boating holiday?

Yes, they got caught on the canal because of all the locks.

Knock, knock
Who's there?
Kenya
Kenya who?
Kenya cook something for Christmas dinner other than Brussels sprouts?

Why does Cuba have such a successful tourism industry?
Because most of the holidaymakers are Havana a good time.

Why did the elephant get charged for luggage on his flight to the Caribbean?
Because he insisted carrying on his trunk.

What does Ant say when getting his house ready for Christmas?
"Dec, the halls with boughs of holly!"

"Did you have a good Easter?"
"Yes, it was eggs-ellent!"

Holidaymaker: "Waiter, will my pizza be long?"
Waiter: "No, Sir, it will be round like everybody else's."

Where would you get spare parts for your yacht at Christmas time?
At the Boxing Day sails, of course!

A tourist visiting Nepal
Wore a dress made of books to the ball
The dress caught on fire
And to her great ire
Burned her contents page, glossary and all!

What is James Bond's favourite Christmas food?
Mince spies.

What says, "Oh, Oh, Oh?"
Father Christmas walking backwards.

What does Dr Who always eat on holiday in Italy?
Dalek bread.

The motor boat Dad uses on holiday is so old, it's insured for fire, scurvy and theft by pirates!

Why did the monster eat the tightrope walker for Christmas dinner?
It wanted a balanced meal.

When on holiday, what's the best day of the week to go to the beach?
Sun-day.

Which Caribbean island attracts the most sheep on holiday?
Baa-Bados.

How do monsters go abroad on holiday?
They fly British Scareways.

Did you know I have travelled to all 12 countries in South America?
I do not Bolivia!

Why can't Christmas trees knit woolly jumpers?
Because they keep on dropping their needles.

What do you call water that washes up on tiny holiday beaches?
Microwaves.

Why was Dr Frankenstein so popular at parties?
He was brilliant at making new friends and quickly had everyone in stitches.

What's a hairdresser's favourite Christmas carol?
Oh, Comb, All Ye Faithful!

Why are a mute Sir Lancelot and a Christmas carol similar?
They're both a Silent Knight.

What does a holidaymaker in Stockholm most like to eat at a Chinese restaurant?
Sweden sour chicken.

Teacher: "We are doing the nativity, Jilly, so why have you brought an ice bucket, a monster and a comedian?"
Jilly: "Because we need presents from the three wise men: cold, Frankenstein and mirth."

What item did the Easter Bunny use after he got wet in the rain?
A hare-dryer.

What do you call the rest Father Christmas takes after delivering all the presents?
A Santa pause.

Patient: "Doctor, on holiday I broke my leg in three places. What do you recommend?"
Doctor: "Never going back to those three places."

What is Tarzan's favourite Christmas song?
Jungle Bells.

What's the most popular visitor attraction for lovers of Italian food?
The Leaning Tower of Pizza.

Why was the advent calendar nervous?
Because its days were numbered.

What shop is the most popular in Britain?
Christmas Tree shops because they have so many branches.

What part of Christmas dinner can tie knots and likes to go camping?
Brussels scouts.

How do vampires sail across the English Channel at Halloween?
In blood vessels.

What comes at the end of Easter Sunday?
The letter y.

Two detectives go on a camping holiday. In the middle of the night, one wakes the other up and says, *"Look up at the sky and tell me what crime has occurred?"*
The second detective is confused. *"I see the stars and the Moon, but no crime."*
The first detective replies, *"Fool, someone has stolen our tent!"*

What do ghosts say when they meet each other on Halloween?
"How do you BOO!"

What sort of car do visitors to Disneyland Paris drive?
A Minnie.

Self-Catering Holidays by Iona Villa

Best Place To Holiday In Europe by Francis Grate

Naturist Holidays by Seymour Bottoms

Camping In Summer by Guy Ropes and Walter Proof

Long Distance Holidays by Farrah Way

Sightseeing On A Tight Budget by Penny Pincher

Enjoy A Spa Holiday by Pam Paired

Holidays In The Far East by Phil E. Peens and Mal Asia

Top Resorts In Spain By Benny Dorm and Ali Kante

SCARY SNIGGERS

Why are all the other numbers afraid of 7?
Because 7 8 9.

What TV quiz show does a vampire with no teeth most like to watch?
Pointless.

Why do skeletons play pianos?
Because they don't have any organs.

What do zombies call small children on skateboards?
Meals on wheels.

Vampires only come out at night
But a vampire tree is quite a sight
It leaves people quite drained
And often deranged
'Cos its bark is as bad as its bite.

Young Witch: "Will I lose my looks as I get older?"
Pupil: "With luck, yes!"

What day of the week do monsters most like to eat small boys and girls?
Chews-day.

What room is missing in a zombie's house?
The living room.

How do witches make sure they use the right ingredients in their potions?
They use their computer's spellchecker, of course!

What do you get if you cross Bambi, a ghost and a gun?
Bam-boo shoots!

Tabitha: "I hear police are looking for a witch with one eye called Wanda."
Jenny: "Really, what's her other eye called?"

Why did the man-eating monster turn vegetarian?
Because he was fed up with people.

In what movie does Dracula battle Luke Skywalker?
The Vampire Strikes Back.

What dinosaur knows more words than any other prehistoric creature?
A thesaurus.

How do you start a letter to a mummy?
Tomb It May Concern.

A vampire who had once been a winner
Was worried at becoming thinner
But when he ordered a meal
What arrived made him squeal,
"Oh, the last thing I want – a stake dinner!"

Why did the dim dinosaur have a short tail?
Because it couldn't remember long stories.

Did you hear about the zombie bike that rode around by itself and ran people over again and again?
Oh yes, it was a vicious cycle.

Patient: "I've heard rumours that you've become a vampire, doctor."
Doctor: "Necks, Please!"

How did the witch prepare for a day at the beach?
She packed plenty of suntan potion and wore her open-toad sandals.

THE GREAT ZOMBIE BAKE OFF

"What is the number one rated TV cookery show amongst crumbling zombies?"
"Break Off!"

"And what are the most popular dishes made on the show?"
"Baked beings in grave-y, a sponge man-wich, and ice scream."

"What time is the show on?"
"Ate o'clock."
"I imagine most zombies are dead tired by then."

"Wasn't the winning zombie's entry, chocolate cornflakes?"
"Yes, he was a dead-icated cereal killer."

127

"Why did two zombies get thrown off the show?"
"One gave everyone a stomach-cake and the other was caught buttering up the judges."

*

Zombie Bob: "Do you still hold your girlfriend's hand?"
Zombie Bill: "Yes, but I wish the rest of her would visit more often."

What are monsters' favourite types of plant?
Ceme-trees.

How do witches travel when their brooms aren't working?
They witch-hike.

Why are candles like witches?
They both tend to be wicked.

Why do aliens go to school on the Sun?
So they can get brighter.

What is a vampire's favourite meal?
Fangers and mash.

Did you hear about the health-freak werewolf that only ate raw, organic vegetables?
Yes, it was the super-natural thing to do.

What is the day called when ghosts play tricks on each other?
April Ghoul's Day.

What sort of shows do ghosts see at the theatre?
Phantomimes.

How does Darth Maul like his toast?
On The Dark Side.

What is Dracula's favourite sport?
Casketball.

"Is Dracula a fan of cricket?"
"I believe so. After all, he turns into a bat every night!"

What happened when the alien spaceship flew too close to the Sun?
It became a frying saucer.

What is the most popular search engine for ghosts?
Ghoul-gle.

Why are ghosts such good teachers?
They go through things over and over again.

Where do ghouls and vampires keep their Halloween savings?
At the blood bank.

An alien from Alpha Centauri
Had ten heads but only the one eye
When he landed on Earth
To everyone's mirth
He had headaches and quickly said, goodbye!

What was Frankenstein's monster's favourite finger food at parties?
Hand-burgers.

And how does he eat them?
He bolts them down.

What special features attract trolls to the Ogre Hotel?
Each room has a rot water bottle and a wide-scream TV.

Dracula: "You not only have bat breath, you're also a pain in the neck!"
Drusilla: "Well, you're so fat, I'm going to call you Draculard!"

Which French skeleton was defeated at the Battle of Waterloo?
Napoleon Boneyparts.

What part of a newspaper do monsters read first?
The horror-scope.

Why did everyone at the spooks and spells fair wear nametags?
So they could tell which witch was which.

What do you call a blind stag ridden by the headless horseman?
No eye deer.

Why did the vampire subscribe to *CBeebies* magazine?
He heard it had a great circulation.

Why was the goalkeeper nicknamed Dracula?
Because he was afraid of crosses.

Daddy Monster: "Your sister makes a lovely stew."
Child Monster: "Yes, but I am going to miss her!"

Why did the referee send the vampire off?
For making biting tackles.

Why are mummies workaholics?
They're wrapped up in their work and don't like to take time off to unwind.

What's the tallest building in Transylvania?

The Vampire State Building.

Where in a football stadium will you often find Dr Jekyll as he turns into Mr Hyde?

In the changing room.

How do you confuse a stupid troll?
Show them into a circular room and tell them their dinner's in the corner.

Why did the ghost get disqualified by the judges on *Strictly Come Dancing*?
Because he was dead on his feet and had no body to dance with.

Knock, knock
Who's there?
Thumping
Thumping who?
Thumping scary just crawled in under your front door!

What do you call the sounds of zombies waking up?
The moaning chorus.

There once was an alien called Zat
Who blasted off into space in his hat
Earth looked, oh so small
But on starting to fall
It looked bigger and BIGGER, then SPLAT!

Why is a child-eating zombie like the letter V?
Because it comes after U.

Ghoul: "I'm off on my summer horrordays tomorrow."
Monster: "Are you going to Boo York?"
Ghoul: "Nope! Try again."
Monster: "Mali-Boo? I got it, Wails!"
Ghoul: "No, Alton Towers."
Monster: "Why there?"
Ghoul: "Because I love going on the roller ghosters!"

What is a witch's favourite bird?
A scare crow.

What do you get if you cross a tortoise with a monster?
A terror-pin.

"Why have you picked a ghost to play in goal?"
"Because I thought the side needed a team spirit."
"Oh well, I guess it might be good having a ghoulkeeper."

How does the abominable snowman travel around the mountains?
By-icicle.

How do monsters keep their breath fresh each morning?
They gargoyle.

What do you call a zombie in a racing car?
A zoom-bie.

What club's application form asks you to write your name, address and blood group?
Dracula's Fang Club.

What do you call a witch that is really nervous and can't stay still?
A twitch.

Why did the undertaker go to the doctors?
He was tired of coffin.

What policeman is in charge of finding and arresting ghosts?
The Detective In-Spectre.

What did the mummy ghost say to her child when getting ready to go out?
"Hurry up and put on your boos and shocks!"

A vampire appeared on TV
And danced into the final with ease
He scored well with his Tango
But his vampire Fangdango
Was so bad, the judge said, "Necks please!"

Strange Bumps In The Night
by Paul Tergeist

Dare You Enter The Haunted House?
by Hugo Furst

Trapped In A Grave
by Berry D'Lythe

We're All Trapped In A Vampire's Lair
by Vic Timms

Ghosts And Ghoulies
by Terry Fayed

The Biggest Zombie Ever
by Hugh Mungus

A Vampire's Terrible Journey
by Helen Bakk

SPORTING SNORTS

Why did the rugby manager bring pencils and paper to the game?
He was hoping his team would draw the match.

How do basketball players stay cool during a hot game?
They sit next to their fans.

Why did the famous golfer wear two pairs of socks?
In case he got a hole in one.

What is Captain Underpants' favourite type of sportsperson?
Boxers.

What do you get if you cross Usain Bolt, a pot of ink and a Boeing 747?
An ink jet sprinter.

What is a ballerina's favourite football score?
Tutu.

What do you call a big bearded snooker player who's a wizard at making big breaks?
Hairy Potter.

I'm not saying our new player is fat, but every time he falls over in a game, he rocks himself to sleep trying to get up!

Athlete: "I cannot see straight."
Optician: "That's because you are suffering from pedestrian eye."
Athlete: "What's that?"
Optician: "Your eyes look both ways before they cross!"

Why did the rugby player's drawing of a square only have three sides?
Because he took a line out.

Did you know that basketball players are some of the only sportspeople that can dribble and still look neat?

What job do out-of-work tennis players most often take?
A waiter or waitress, because they serve so well.

"I had to return the Losers United FC darts to the club shop."

"*Why?*"

"They didn't have any points."

What's the smelliest sport in the world?

Ping pong.

I hear gymnasts are really kind and helpful.

Yes, they'd bend over backwards for anyone.

Why was Laura Kenny unable to win the cycling gold medal?

Because her bike was two tyre-d.

What sportsperson is warmest during winter time?

A long jumper.

What is golfer Rory McIlroy's favourite mealtime?

Tee.

If you have umpires in cricket and referees in football, what do you have in bowls?

Ice-cream, of course!

What did the archer get when he hit a bullseye?

A very angry bull.

Dad: "Sorry to hear the local skatepark closed down, Son."

Son: "It's awful. I'm so skate-bored!"

Did you hear about cricket star Joe Root doing poorly on a TV quiz show?

Yes, he was stumped by the questions.

Coach: "Why are you running to your left and right instead of straight ahead?"
Athlete: "It's these tablets I am taking, Coach. They have side effects!"

Did you hear about the snooker player arrested for cheating?
Yes, the police said he had jumped the cue and pocketed the cash.

And did you hear what happened next? He said he'd been framed and then escaped!
You mean, he made a break for it?

Sports reporter: "And what gear were you in, Chris Froome, when you crashed during the bike race?"
Chris Froome: "Oh, the usual, cycling shorts, shirt and a helmet."

Why do you call your football club's new striker "Ceasefire"?
Because he's not taken any shots.

What drink should you avoid at a party for boxers?
The punch.

What was the nickname of the giant who was a terrible cricket fielder?
Fe Fi Fo Fumble.

Did you hear about the two hugely overweight players on their first day back in training?
One trained in short bursts and the other trained in burst shorts.

What happened to the naughty tennis player?
He got sent to court.

Knock, knock
Who's there?
Chile
Chile who?
Chile being a downhill skier with no clothes on!

What is the hardest part of parkour freerunning?
The ground.

Did you hear about the silly rugby player who installed a skylight in his expensive apartment?
The people in the flat above were furious.

There was a footballer from Clyde
Who blasted a penalty wide
In the next game, his son
Well, he also missed one
And now neither can get in the side.

Where do ghosts hold their swimming competitions?
In the Dead Sea.

Why was the hockey pitch so wet and soggy?
Because the players kept dribbling all over it.

"Oi, Sergio," shouted the angry manager in the dressing room. "You were terrible today. You're a disgrace to the team."
"Don't listen to him," said a team-mate afterwards, trying to cheer Sergio up. "He doesn't know what he's talking about. He only repeats what everybody else says!"

What was Mo Farah's favourite subject at school?
Jog-graphy.

How did the hockey pitch end up in the shape of a triangle?
Because a player took a corner.

Why did Andy Murray get told off by his neighbours?
Because he was making a racket.

Which basketball player can jump higher than a house?
All of them – houses can't jump!

What do you call a *Star Wars* baddie who's afraid to go into the boxing ring?
A Sith-y.

Why did the silly angler wear a suit of armour?
Because he thought he was entering a knight fishing competition.

In the World Cup, a player called Quinn
Who was so incredibly thin
Tried to drink lemonade
But I'm terribly afraid
He' slipped through the straw and fell in.

Which athletics event did the church vicar win easily?

The steeplechase.

"I'll never marry a tennis player."

"Why not?"

"Well, to them love means nothing."

What sort of injury do most field athletes suffer?

A slipped discus.

Why are baseball and a fish and chip shop similar?

Both rely on good batters.

Why did the Olympian carry a hammer, nails and a tin of creosote?
He wanted to have a go at fencing.

What object do boxers keep all their tickets and memorabilia in?
A scrap book.

What did the athletics coach and a handyman have in common?
They both use drills.

What sort of dinosaur won the Golden Boot for most football goals struck?
A Tyranno-score-us.

Did you hear the bad news about the former champion slalom skier?
Yes, I hear he's gone downhill.

A defender who played for Chard
Was famous for being rock hard
His tackles it seemed
Were a bit too extreme
As the ref showed him 50 red cards!

The Black Sea and the Mediterranean Sea had a race. Who won?
Neither, they tide.

Why did the canoe champion and a fan watching online both give up?
Neither could get a good stream.

What is a boxer's favourite part of a joke?

The punch line, of course!

Knock, knock

Who's there?

Dozen

Dozen who?

Dozen anyone play rugby in your house?

Did you hear about the marathon runner who wore bad fitting shoes and came in last?

He really suffered the agony of de-feet!

Why could the martial arts competitor not take part in the tournament?

She was suffering from Kung Flu.

Why did the wrestler bring a bunch of keys into the ring?
So he could get himself out of a headlock.

Dad: "How's your trampolining at gym club going?"
Daughter: "Oh, up and down."

Why did the policemen arrest the baseball player?
Because he stole third base.

How does Usain Bolt get online and keep up with his social media?
He logs on to the Sprinternet.

What name do you call a rugby pitch groundsman?
Doug.

Why did the strongman pause before lifting the barbell?
Because he liked to make the audience weight.

How did the surfer greet people on the beach?
He waved.

What is Anthony Joshua and Amir Khan's favourite part of Christmas?
Boxing Day, of course!

What football club is the best at connecting computers?
Leeds.

What are gymnasts' favourite desserts?
Splits.

Why was Cinderella so bad at hockey?
She kept running away from the ball.

An excited young footballer goes up to his coach and says: "Coach, Madchester Rovers wants me to play for them very badly."
The coach replies: "Well, you're just the boy for the job!"

What's the name of a man who loves long walks in the countryside?
Ike.

Coach: "Why didn't you stop the ball?"
Hockey goalkeeper: "I thought that's what the net was for."

FOOTBALL
FUNNIES

FOOTBALL PLAYERS

Manager: "I call our striker, Dane Mooney, my £10 million wonder player."
Reporter: "Why?"
Manager: "Because every time he plays and misses a goal, I wonder why I paid £10 million for him!"

A manager is interviewing a possible new player for his team and asks: "Do you kick with both feet?"
"Don't be silly," replies the player. "If I did that, I wouldn't be able to stand up, would I?"

"Our new Spanish midfielder is so keen on staying fit that he works carrying bricks on a building site during the summer."
"I didn't know that. What's his name again?"
"Manuel Labour!"

What do Lionel Messi and a magician have in common?
Both are good at hat tricks.

Terrible midfielder: "Boss, I've got a fab idea for making the team better."
Manager: "Great, I didn't know you were leaving!"

Our new striker, Edmundo Cesar Lorenzo Farrincha Gonzalez De Sousa, incurred quite a transfer fee last year.
And that was just for his name on the back of the shirt!

A brilliant young player called Paul
Was also terribly tall
One night while in bed
He stretched out his leg
And turned off the light in the hall.

There once was a player from Reading
Who tripped and fell over some bedding
His head really swelled
But he smiled and he yelled,
"Great! This will help me with heading!"

A striker who played for United
Turned out to be very short-sighted
With great ball control
He scored an own goal
And the other team's fans were delighted.

Reporter: "What happened when the world's smallest man joined your team?"
Manager: "We played the game a man short."

Why did the foolish footballer take his pillow and blanket out into the woods?
So he could sleep like a log.

The head coach of the town's struggling football team was walking down the street when he saw an old lady puffing as she dragged her shopping bags along. He stopped and asked her, "Can you manage?"

She replied, "Of course I can, but you got yourself into this mess. Don't ask me to sort it out!"

In football, what's harder to catch the faster you run?

Your breath.

Why didn't the short midfielder need much sleep?

He was never long in bed.

Which player would you not want to share a room with?

Lionel Messi.

Why did Cinderella not improve as a footballer?

Because her coach turned into a pumpkin.

What do you get if you cross a football player with a mythical creature that has the head of a man and the body of a horse?

A centaur forward.

FOOTBALL TEAMS

When our new manager said he thought our team would finish second this season, I thought he meant in the league.

I didn't realise that he meant in every single game!

Why did Turkey get the most yellow cards?

Because the referee felt they made the most fowl tackles.

Which English football team likes ice cream the most?
Aston Vanilla.

What is a snake's favourite football team?
Slitherpool.

What's the difference between my football team and a tea bag?
The tea bag stays in the cup longer.

Which side did Shy Barry, Quiet Steve and Wouldn't-Say-Boo-To-A-Goose Gordon all play for?
The reserve-d team.

What colour football kit did the shoutiest and mouthiest team in the league wear?
Yeller!

What football team does the demolition man like to support?
Wrexham.

Snow White goes searching for the football-mad Seven Dwarfs who are believed to be lost in a cave.
Reaching the cave's entrance, she shouts down, *"Who will win the World Cup this year?"*
From deep within the cave comes the reply, *"England!"*
"Ah," **says Snow White,** *"At least Dopey is still alive!"*

A winger was poetry in motion
But his retirement caused a commotion
He stopped playing, they say,
Two months before May
And his team missed out on promotion.

Which national team's footballers cannot wait for lunch or dinner-time after training?
Hungary.

Filthy thieves have stolen the team bath at Arsenal's Emirates Stadium.
Police believe they made a clean getaway.

I hear Oxo are bringing out a new gravy cube in Liverpool colours.
It's called Laughing Stock and crumbles under pressure.

Our new striker is scoring hatfuls of goals in training. Then again, it's not much of a surprise. After all, he is playing against his own team's defence!

"How come you have so much spare time?"
"Well, I work 8 hours a day and sleep 8 hours a day. That leaves me 16 hours to do what I want."
"Hang on. There aren't 32 hours in a day."
"But my job is to guard the Arsenal trophy cabinet, so I can sleep and work at the same time!"

Two football fans were walking through a cemetery when they saw a tombstone that read:

"Here lies Jack Carter – a good man and a Chelsea fan."
One turned to the other and asked,
"When did they start putting two people in one grave?"

GOALKEEPERS AND GOALS

What type of footballer do bank managers like the most?
Goalkeepers. They're the best savers.

What do you call a girl who stands inside the goalposts and stops the ball rolling away?
Annette.

"I've been asked to sign up as the new goalkeeper for the Circus Clown FC team."
"As an amateur?"
"No, it's a fool-time job!"

Assistant coach: "Our new striker's terrible, boss. I thought you said he eats, drinks and sleeps football."

Head coach: "Yes, he does . . . he just can't play it!"

"Our new goalkeeper has just been nicknamed 'Jigsaw'."
"Why's that?"
"Because every time the other team attacks, he falls to pieces."

A veteran goalie named Keith
Mislaid his set of false teeth
When he sat down at training
He soon leapt up, exclaiming:
"I've just been bitten beneath!"

Mary had a little lamb
Who played in goal a lot.
It let in lots and lots of goals,
So now it's in the pot.

What's a goalkeeper's favourite meal?
Beans on post.

A goalie let in six goals in each of his last three games. Worrying about how badly he's been playing, he goes to see his doctor.
"Your problem is you've got two left feet," **diagnoses the doctor.**
"I'd like a second opinion," **insists the goalie.**
"Okay. You're useless, too!" **replies the doctor.**

Why was the goalkeeper always at the laundrette?
He was hoping to get more clean sheets.

What's the difference between a terrible goalkeeper and a taxi cab driver?
A taxi cab driver only lets four in at a time.

What happened to the footballer who took a penalty just as heavy fog filled the ground?

He mist.

REFEREES AND MANAGERS

Where do the chairmen of football clubs go in their grounds during a dull 0-0 draw?

The Bored Room.

Why was the manager happy to be caught speeding by the traffic police?

He was delighted to get three points.

Why did the struggling manager shake the club cat?

To see if there was any money for transfers left in the kitty.

Player to manager: "I know I wasn't at my best today, but I don't think I deserve a mark of 0 out of 10 for my performance."

Manager to player: "Neither do I, but it's the lowest mark I can give."

The new manager of our struggling football team is strict and won't stand any nonsense. Last Saturday, he caught two fans climbing over the stadium wall and was angry with them. He grabbed them and said, "Get back in there and watch the game until it finishes!"

A referee shows a yellow card to a player for a bad foul and says, "Ronnie, you really must learn how to give and take."

The player replies, "But I have, Ref. I gave him a kick and took his legs away!"

Assistant coach: "That new player you've signed only weighs 30kg and only has a 22-inch waist. Where did you get him from?"
Manager: "Finland!"

Referee to a player: "I hope I don't see you cheating."
Player to referee: "I hope you don't see either, Ref!"

Referee: "I'm sending you off."
Player: "What for?"
Referee: "For the rest of the match, dummy!"

What colour is a referee's favourite whistle?
Blew.

What is a referee's favourite drink?
Penal-tea.

FANS AND FOOTBALL GROUNDS

A not-too-bright football fan arrives really late and takes his seat during the second half of the game. *"What's the score?"* **he asks as he sits down.** *"Nil-Nil,"* **the person next to him replies.**
"And what was the score at half-time?"

Which month of the football season has 28 days?
All of them . . . idiot!

A football fan hands over £40 to the ticket office at Stoke City FC and says, "Two please."
The ticket person replies, "Will that be defenders or strikers, Sir?"

A pound coin was thrown onto the pitch at my struggling football club. Police are trying to work out whether it was thrown by a hooligan or if it was actually a takeover bid!

Two fans are in the queue to get into the grounds . . .
"I wish I'd brought my bedroom table to the stadium."
"Why would you do that?"
"Because I left our tickets on it."

"I hear they're making improvements for the fans at your ground . . . They're turning all the seats round so that they face away from the pitch!"

What runs along a football pitch but never moves?
A sideline.

Why can't I buy a tea or coffee at this football ground?
Because all the mugs are on the pitch and all the cups are in other teams' trophy cabinets!

A football fan appears in court charged with throwing something into the river.
Judge: "And what did you throw?"
Fan: "Wood."
Judge: "Well, that's not much of a crime, is it?"
Lawyer: "Ahem, your lordship, Wood was the referee."

A man knocked on the door and was asking for donations for his football club's new swimming pool.
So, I gave him a glass of water.

Why is an orchestra conductor like 20,000 fans leaving a stadium at the end of a match?
Because they both know the score.

MATCHES AND COMPETITIONS

Where do Champions League players like to have a dance?
At the Champions League Foot Ball, of course!

"Oh, I could kick myself," said the striker after failing to score another simple chance.
"Don't bother," replied his captain. "You'd only miss!"

Why isn't the England team allowed to have a dog at football tournaments?
Because it can't hold on to a lead.

Which country at the World Cup has the most slippery attackers?
Greece.

What's the difference between a blunt needle and the worst team in the league?

Nothing. They're both pointless.

Why are the players in my football team like cannons in a battle in every match they play?

Because they keep on getting fired.

My team has lost all 11 games in the league, so what's the difference between them and a toothpick?

The toothpick has two points.

Which is the coldest country to take part in the World Cup?

Chile.

What's the loudest noise after England take part in a World Cup penalty shootout?
Their opponents laughing.

Which World Cup team's players never carry any cash with them?
The Czechs.

What ship holds 20 teams but only three leave it each season?
The Premiership.

What's the Spanish team's favourite scoreline?
Juan-Nil to them!

It looks like FC Trifle are going down this season."
"Yes, they're going to be jelly-gated!"

Which team is always there at the end of the match?

The Finnish team.

Which team were Lunar League champions?

Bayern Moonick.

Football pundits estimate that struggling team Hapless FC will last three seasons in the Premier League . . .

Autumn, Winter and Spring!

Football Conditions in Brazil in Summer
by Gloria Swether

The Bad Shot by Misty Target

Disaster in Defence by Owen Goal

Zero Out of Ten: Rating the Worst Teams of All Time
by A. Pauline Marx

Hurricane Hits Stadium
by Rufus Blownoff

Cheered Off The Pitch
by Stan D. Novation

Famous English Football Grounds
by Emma Rates and Anne Field

Best Seats in the Stadium
by Sue Perview

When Fans Snub Stadiums by M. T. Ground

Washing Smelly Football Kit
by Dee Tergent

A Who's Who of Football
by Hugh Didwatt

The Day My Football Shorts Fell Down
by Lou Selastic

HI-TECH
HUMOUR

What did the old broken-down computer ask another computer?

"Can I crash at your place?"

Why was the party on Mars so terrible?

Because it lacked atmosphere.

What happens when you put fruit and sugar instead of toner into a laser printer?

You get a paper jam.

How did the computer hacker get out of prison?

He used the Escape key.

When hungry, what is astronaut Tim Peake's favourite part of the day?

Launch time.

What amazing computer software allows you to see through walls?
Windows.

Which pantomime character do you find on a computer?
Buttons.

What do you call someone who spends 24 hours a day on social media?
Anything you like, they're not listening to you anyway.

Did you get the link to the boomerang club on Facebook?
Yes, and I return to it again and again.

What did the social media addict do on Halloween?
He went trick or tweeting.

Which make of computer is the best at singing pop songs?
A Dell.

How do dirty astronauts get clean?
They take a meteor shower.

Why is a church like a computer text document?
They both use fonts.

How does a tree get Internet access?
It logs on.

Where would you find black holes?
At the end of black socks.

What happened when the two webpage developers met?
It was love at first site.

188

Schoolboy: "Why do computers and printers hum, Sir?"
Computer teacher: "Because they don't know the words!"

Why is a social media addict the opposite of a man who owes lots of money?
One checks Facebook all the time but the other cannot face his chequebook.

Which planet needs the biggest jewellery box?
Saturn, because it has lots of rings.

Lamb 1: "What is your favourite smartphone app?"
Lamb 2: "Sorry to say, it's Ewe-Tube."
Lamb 1: "There's no need to be sheepish about it!"

What music do astronauts on the International Space Station listen to?
Nep-tunes.

Where do old computers go to party and boogie?
The floppy disc-o.

My computer's got the Bad-Goalie Virus.
It can't save anything.

Why was the laptop shivering at night?
Because it had forgotten to close all the windows.

What runs but doesn't get anywhere?
A computer program.

Why did the online spider get a pair of glasses?
To improve its websight.

Why did the river get rich?
It opened its own streaming service.

What website does Chewbacca use to learn about things?
Wookiee-pedia.

Why is a deleted social media account like a bowl of breakfast cereal?
Because it's full of shredded tweets.

Did you hear about the killer robot which had its limbs removed?
Yes, I hear it's now 'armless.

What sort of smartphone photos do Santa's helpers take of themselves?
Elfies.

How do astronauts see in the darkness of space?
They use satel-lights.

What is a Nintendo Wii called in France?
A Nintendo Yes.

Knock, knock
Who's there?
Jupiter
Jupiter who?
Jupiter virus on my computer? You swine!

How do you get a Squirtle and a Pikachu on to a crowded bus?
You poke 'em on!

What is Sonic the Hedgehog's favourite season of the year?
Spring.

A coder was working one night
When he got a terrible fright
A bug in his PC
Seemed to be hungry
As the bug gave the PC a byte!

What do you say to a computer game character who is late for his holiday?

"Pack, man!"

Why did the kid who loved flying robots always bore people?

Because he droned on such a lot.

What driver never starts their car or gets a parking ticket?

A screw-driver.

What sort of games console do witches use to play World of Warcraft?

A Hexbox 360.

What was the problem with the new Titanic smartphone?

It kept syncing all the time.

Where do honey makers sell their jars online?
Bee-bay.

What did the computer technician give the gamer whose computer had a virus?
A tablet.

Dad: "You really shouldn't code programs when you should be sleeping, Son."
Son: "Yes, you're right. I might get a bed bug!"

"Did you hear they're making a Minecraft movie?"
"I bet it will be a block-buster!"

Why does my mobile sting me each time it rings?
Because it's a smart phone.

What do you call a policeman listening to music on his MP3 player?
An iPlod.

Which part of a mobile phone finds texting really tedious?
The key-bored.

How much do dead batteries cost?
Nothing. They're free of charge.

Why was the old computer proud of the newest PC?
Because it was a microchip off the old block.

What happens when you take your laptop with you when you go ice skating?
You get a slipped disk.

What did the building block say to the robot gripper?
"Lego, you're hurting me!"

Did you see the new optician's webpage on your iPad?
Yes, it's definitely a site for sore eyes!

Who was the first detective to investigate electricity?
Sherlock Ohms.

What did the astronaut on the Moon do when he trod on another astronaut's foot?
He Apollo-gised.

"Do you know what my smartwatch does when it's hungry?"
"No?"
"It goes back for seconds!"

Air Traffic Control: "Hi there Captain Johnson, can you give me your height and position?"
Pilot: "I'm 1.8 metres and sitting down in my plane's cockpit!"

Why is a frequent smartphone user just like the captain of the Starship Enterprise?
They both rely on Data.

What sort of poetry do astronauts on the International Space Station most enjoy?
Uni-verses.

Did you find the police chat group online?
Yes, but I didn't find it very arresting.

What do you call a spacecraft with all its seats and fittings stripped out?
A Sparse Shuttle.

Why is a badly written computer program just like an outbreak of sickness?
Because they are both full of bugs.

Have you seen the new Velcro website?
Yes, I couldn't tear myself away from it!

Geek Gina: "I sent you a link to garbage-dump.co.uk. What do you think?"
Geek Gemma: "I thought it was a load of rubbish!"

Have you visited that webpage about shipwrecks I told you about?
Yes, but it hasn't really sunk in yet.

Which lady is in charge of handing out website domain names?
Dot Comm.

Where do space probes dock when they visit another planet?
At parking meteors.

Why is the Internet similar to a golf course on a beginner's open day?
They're both full of hackers.

Jackie: "I've been on my laptop computer all night."
Jenny: "Wouldn't you have been more comfortable on a mattress like everyone else?"

"All the books in my bedroom fell down and smashed my smartphone!"
"Oh, no!"
"Still, I only have my shelf to blame!"

What cartoon show do smartphones most like to watch?
The SIM-sons.

How do you make a convoy of *Star Wars* robots pick a new route to travel along?
You make an R2-Detour.

How do ghouls run apps on their smartphones?

They use the smartphone's touchscream.

Hipster Hal: "Hey, man, do you want to borrow my cool pocket calculator?"

Hipster Harry: "No thanks, I already know how many pockets I have!"

How did the King send a message on social media about his new castle?

He sent a moat-ification.

How does Bill Gates cool down the rooms of his mansion?

He clicks on an icon and Windows open.

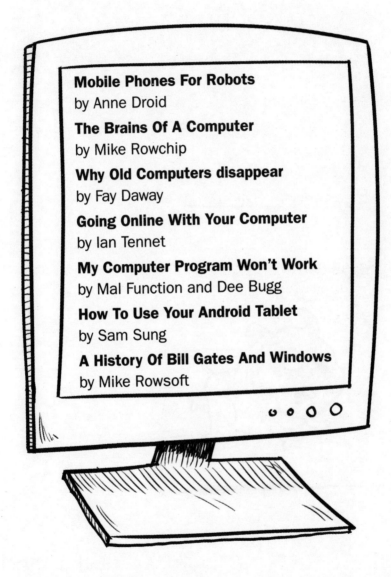

Mobile Phones For Robots
by Anne Droid

The Brains Of A Computer
by Mike Rowchip

Why Old Computers disappear
by Fay Daway

Going Online With Your Computer
by Ian Tennet

My Computer Program Won't Work
by Mal Function and Dee Bugg

How To Use Your Android Tablet
by Sam Sung

A History Of Bill Gates And Windows
by Mike Rowsoft

PET PUNS

What goes squeak, dot, dash, dot, squeak?
Mouse code.

Why was the pet tarantula found using a computer?
He was searching the web.

What's green, squawks and jumps out of aircraft?
A parrot-trooper.

Where did the pet rabbit go to spend its birthday money?
The hopping centre.

What do young dogs eat when they go to the cinema?
Pup-corn.

What animal do you get if you cross a pig with a fir tree?
A pork-u-pine.

Why can grass be so dangerous to your pet?
Because it is full of blades.

Teacher: "You can't bring your pet skunk into school, Olivia, what about the terrible smell?"
Olivia: "Oh, I am sure it'll get used to it."

What's a horse's favourite sport?
Stable Tennis.

What do you call a cat that has swallowed a whole duck?
A duck-filled fatty puss.

Why was the dog with the very small bottom always late?

He was a little behind.

How do bunny rabbits keep fit?

They go to hare-obics classes.

Why did the sheepdog crash the tractor?

He was trying to make a ewe turn.

What does a cat use for oral hygiene?
Mousewash.

What do you call an Alsatian that wears a Fit Bit on its leg?
A smart watch dog.

What dog patrols the boundary between England and Wales?
A Border Collie.

"My dog is a nuisance. He chases everyone on a bicycle. What can I do?"
"Take his bicycle away!"

What do you get if you cross a cat with a lemon?
A sourpuss.

Did you hear about the Labrador that ate a lamp?
It wanted a light snack.

What do you call a pet duck that flies with an axe?
A lumber-quack.

What's the name of the coy carp who was a secret agent?
James Pond.

What happened when the female cat swallowed a ball of wool?
She had a litter of mittens.

Boy: "I'd like to buy a book on raising pet tortoises?"
Bookseller: "May I ask why?"
Boy: "I dropped mine down a mineshaft by mistake!"

"Where does your pet horse live?"
"In the neigh-bourhood."

What sort of pictures does your talented pet cat paint?
Paw-traits, mainly.

"Is it true you bought a present of pure gold for your pet rabbit?"
"Nope, but I did buy it 24 carrots!"

What did the Yorkshire terrier say after he'd been covered in mite powder?
"Long time, no flea!"

Why are birds the richest creatures on the planet?
Because they invested in the stork market.

Why did the cat delight the optician?
Because it had purr-fect eyesight.

What's a cat's favourite breakfast cereal?
Mice Krispies.

Alfie: "I hear goldfish are easy to weigh."
Pet shop owner: "Yes, they come with their own scales!"

What do you call a boat that contains lots of decks with tanks of coy carp?
A multi-story carp ark.

Which American president was fond of keeping furry pets?
Abrahamster Lincoln.

Bob: "The bees in our hive are sick, where should I take them?"
Todd: "I suggest the waspital."

How can you tell which end of a worm is which?
Tickle its middle and see which end giggles.

Why are cats so brilliant at computer gaming?
Because they've got nine lives and can paws the game any time they like.

What do you give a pet budgie that isn't well?
Tweetment.

"Hey, my pet snake was found lying on your brother's car!"
"Really? I thought it was a windscreen viper."

Where do hamsters go on city breaks?

Hamsterdam.

What is a tortoise's favourite sport?

Terrapin bowling.

Is it bad luck if a black cat follows you?

That depends on whether you're a man or a mouse.

Son: "Dad, my pet pig is sick, what should I do?"

Dad: "Go to the medicine cabinet and get the oink-ment."

What drinks milk, purrs and has 12 legs?

Three cats.

What sort of horses scare people at night?
Night-mares.

What is a cat's favourite sports car?
A Fur-rari.

Why is a thirsty cat like Mo Farah?
He keeps going back for one more lap.

How did the cat keep order amongst all the other pets?
He used claw enforcement.

What illness do most birds suffer from?
Flew.

What side of a guinea pig has the most fur?
The outside.

What do budgies eat for breakfast?
Tweetabix.

Did you hear about the cat that drank a whole bottle of milk in just 30 seconds?
He set a new lap record.

What do you call a cat with eight legs?
An octo-puss.

What athletics event are parrots good at?
Polly vaulting.

What TV soap do horses and ponies like the most?
Neigh-bours.

What do you call the three swordfighting mice?
The Three Mouseketeers.

And what happened to them when they got trapped in a freezer?
They became mice cubes.

Who won the fight between the hedgehog and the tortoise?
The hedgehog, on points.

What did the mouse say after it took a shower under the garden sprinkler?
"I feel squeaky clean!"

Ginny: "What should I do with my pet frog? He is terribly ill."
Amelia: "Best get to the vets for a hoperation."

What happened to the mice when a lock had been put on the fridge door?
They were cheesed off!

What breed of dog loves bath times?
A sham-poodle.

What do two families of warring mice send each other on December 25th?

Cross Mouse cards.

What do you get if you cross a dog with an aeroplane?

A jet setter.

Why do guinea pigs have fur coats?
Because when they wore kagouls, the mice and hamsters laughed at them.

Why did the owner put his dog's steak dinner on top of the fridge?
Because the dog was on a high protein diet.

Where would you find the brainiest fish?
In a think tank.

Where do you take your pet rabbit to be groomed?
A hare-dresser.

"I'm very worried about our cat, Monty. He has swallowed three coins."
"I'm sorry to hear that. But at least now there's some cash in the kitty!"

Where do hungry cats dream of going on holiday?
The Canary Islands.

What do you call the heaviest mouse in the world?
A hippopota-mouse.

Why are an ocean scientist and an excited puppy similar?
One tags a whale and the other wags his tail.

Jeff: "What do you get if you cross a pig with my pet millipede?"
Gemma: "I don't know."
Jeff: "Bacon and legs!"

What do you get if you cross a sheepdog and a rose?
A collie-flower.

How did the Labrador dog plan out his painting?

By making a ruff sketch, first.

Ten Years With My Pet Rat
by Annie Versary

The Friendly Pet Shop
by Juana Iguana

Who Let The Cat Out?
by Doris O'Penn

Keeping Predatory Fish
by Barack Oooda

Dinners For Dogs
by Nora Bone

PLANT AND CREATURE CHUCKLES

What did one tree say to another when woodpeckers pecked holes in its trunk?
"I'm bored!"

Why did the farmer use a plant to connect to the Internet?
Because he thought it would make a good router.

What do you call a fish listening to music on an MP3 player?
An iCod.

Which Middle Eastern country do sheep like to travel to?
Baa-rain.

What did the giant oak say when the lumberjack chopped off its branch?
"I've just become an ampu-tree!"

What happened when the giant duck jumped up and down 10 times?
It caused a giant earth-quack.

Did you see the fruit bat?
No, but I think I saw the salad bowl!

Why did the dolphin blush?
Because it saw the boat's bottom.

What website do cows use to watch videos?
Moo-tube.

Where do otters keep their valuables?
In the river bank.

Where do lions most like to dance?
At a meatball.

**Which predator eats other creatures
two-by-two?**
Noah's shark.

**What's purple, fruity and yells for
help from the top of a castle tower?**
A damson in distress.

What is an eagle's favourite TV show?
Britain's Got Talons.

Where can you find out how heavy a blue whale is?
At the whale-weigh station.

What animals are brilliant on the trapeze and at performing somersaults?
Acro-bats.

Did you hear about the maths teacher's plant in his classroom?
Yes, it had square roots.

What do you get if you cross a harp player with a hen?
A chicken that plucks itself.

What is a microbe's favourite TV soap drama?
Yeast-enders.

Auntie: "Did you like the plant I sent you?"
Niece: "Not at first, but it's growing on me!"

What sort of music do flower growers most like?
Heavy petal.

Knock, knock
Who's there?
Alpaca
Alpaca who?
Alpaca the suitcase, we're late for our flight!

Did you hear about the man who captured hyenas in a wooden vat?
He had a barrel of laughs!

Where do giant killer plants play football?
Old Triffid.

What do you get if you cross a cow with a trampoline?

A milkshake.

"Have you seen the man-eating crocodile?"

"No, but I have seen the man eating chicken. He's over there!"

What did the bee say when it struck a goal in hockey?

"Hive scored!"

Why was the fox going, "Oink! Moo! Baa!"

It was at school learning foreign languages.

What fruit is brilliant at fixing leaking taps and pipes?

A plum-er.

Why did the pig give up running the marathon on the hottest day of the year?
He was bacon in the heat.

How do you turn a fox into a male cow?
Take away the "f".

What do you get if you cross ladybirds with a rabbit?
Bugs bunny.

Why were the elephants thrown out of the swimming pool?
Because they couldn't keep their trunks up.

What ballet do pigs in tutus perform?
Swine Lake.

Why did your sister become a fruit picker?
Well, she said it was a plum job and she's getting a raisin a few weeks' time!

What bird is found at every mealtime?
A swallow.

Why did the tree make a terrible worker?
It wooden do what it was told to.

What tree can't you climb at a football ground?
A lavatory.

What happened to the skunk when it let off a bad smell on the soccer pitch?
It was scent off.

Why was the African Game Reserve football team banned?
It was found to be full of cheetahs.

What do you call a male cow that's snoring?
A bull-dozer.

Did you hear about the body-building cattle rancher?
Yes, I heard he had very strong calves.

Lynne: "How does a hippopotamus hide in a cherry tree?"
Nigel: "It paints its hoof nails red!"
Lynne: "That's ridiculous."
Nigel: "Have you ever seen a hippo in a cherry tree?"
Lynne: "Nope."
Nigel: "Aha! Shows you how well it works."

What football team do most cows support?
Uddersfield Town.

What snake is the best at arithmetic?
An adder.

Why did the sea bird appear tired out?
Because it was a puffin.

What do you call a mad mite on the Moon?
A Lunar-tick.

Oscar: "Wow, all those sheep have been clipped to look exactly the same."
Ama: "Yes, it must be shear coincidence!"

If an elephant sits down on an ant, what sport is he playing?
Squash.

What do you call a snake that works for the government?
A civil serpent.

Which insect doesn't make a great goalkeeper?
The fumble bee.

At which ground do spiders play football?
Webley Stadium.

Why did the giant male pig have no friends in the sty?
Because he was the world's biggest boar.

Why couldn't the gorilla take part in the London Marathon?
Because it wasn't part of the human race.

Which pop singer do you get if you cross a clothes-maker with a fast bird?
Taylor Swift.

What fruit do you get if you cross a fir tree with an iPad?
A pine-apple.

Why did the spider carry a tiny computer with it as it hunted for prey?
So it could search the web.

What is the name of the social media site used by lions and tigers?
Fiercebook.

Why did the leopard wear a striped onesie?
So that it wouldn't be spotted.

What sort of social media do crocodiles most like to use?
Snapchat.

Where do polar bears go to party?
To the snowball.

How do you make a giant squid giggle?
Give him ten tickles.

Knock, knock
Who's there?
Police
Police who?
Police open the door, there's a swarm of bees out here!

A grizzly bear walks into a restaurant and orders.
Bear: "I would like a hamburger .... and fries."
Waiter: "Why the big pause?"
Bear: "I don't know, I was born this way!"

Did you hear Farmer Giles' strange talk about milking cows?
Yes, it was udder nonsense.

Why did the centipede turn up late for the football match?
It took two hours to tie all the laces on his football boots.

Why did all the pigs in the football team stand to attention before the game started?
Because the band started playing the National Hamthem.

Did you see the young, romantic chickens at the ball?
Yes, they were dancing chick-to-chick.

What has antlers and sucks blood?
A moose-quito.

Did you hear about the hottest country in the world?
Yes, the cows there give off evaporated milk!

How do you stop moles digging up your garden?
Take away their spades.

What does a bee use to style its hair?
A honey-comb.

Why do shrimp play all their tennis at the back of the court?
Because they don't like going near nets.

Why do young polar bears eat seal meat and blubber?
You'd cry if you had to eat seal!

What's the difference between an injured tiger and a wet day?
One pours with rain whilst the other roars with pain.

What's a snake's favourite school subject?
Hisssssss-tory.

What is a wildebeest's favourite TV comedy show?
Have I Got Gnus For You.

What time is it when all the bees fly home?
Hive o'clock.

What type of bird is terrible at heading a football?
Duck.

Did you hear about the marsupial who tried to get a job in Australia?
It failed because it didn't have the right koalafications.

What monkey can fly?
A hot air baboon.

What do you call a grizzly that's really flexible?
Yoga Bear.

What did the sea bass say as it performed a magic trick?

"Pick a cod, any cod."

Where does a cheetah get its meals from when visiting a city?

From fast-food outlets.